Perfect Pumpkins

By Jeff Bauer

SCHOLASTIC INC.

NEW YORK • TORONTO • LONDON • AUCKLAND • SYDNEY
MEXICO CITY • NEW DELHI • HONG KONG • BUENOS AIRES

ISBN: 0-439-87639-7

Photo Credits
Cover: Andy Caulfield/The Image Bank/Getty Images; title page: Marc Moritsch/National Geographic/Getty Images; contents page, top: Lori Adamski Peek/Stone/Getty Images; contents page, center: Robert J. Erwin/Photo Researchers, Inc.; contents page, bottom: SW Productions/Photodisc Green/Getty Images; page 4: Lori Adamski Peek/Stone/Getty Images; page 5: Craig Lovell/Corbis; page 6: Bettmann/Corbis; page 6 inset: Edward Kinsman/Photo Researchers, Inc.; page 7: E.R. Degginger/Photo Researchers, Inc.; page 7, inset: John Kaprielian/Photo Researchers, Inc.; page 8: Robert J. Erwin/Photo Researchers, Inc.; page 9, top: Scott Camazine/Photo Researchers, Inc.; page 9, bottom: John Kaprielian/Photo Researchers, Inc.; page 10: John Kaprielian/Photo Researchers, Inc.; page 11: Carol Mallory/Dembinsky Photo Associates (DPA); page 12: SW Productions/Photodisc Green/Getty Images; page 13: Ryan McVay/Photodisc Green/Getty Images; page 14: Lorry Eason/Digital Vision/Getty Images; page 15: Photodisc Blue/Getty Images; back cover: Marc Moritsch/National Geographic/Getty Images.

Photo research by Sarah Longacre
Design by Holly Grundon

12 11 10 9 8 7 6 5 4 3 2 1 6 7 8 9 10 11/0

Printed in the U.S.A.
First printing, September 2006

Contents

Chapter 1
All About Pumpkins
Page 4

Chapter 2
Growing Pumpkins
Page 8

Chapter 3
Pumpkin Treats
Page 12

Glossary and Comprehension Questions
Page 16

Chapter 1

All About Pumpkins

Do you know what is great about pumpkins? Every pumpkin is different. Take a peek!

Pumpkins can be tall or short. They can be smooth or bumpy or round or **lopsided**!

This little white pumpkin is called a "Baby Boo."

Pumpkins can be small or big. This little white pumpkin weighs less than one pound. This giant orange pumpkin weighs 450 pounds!

These tiny pumpkin seeds can grow into big pumpkins.

Do you know what is inside of a pumpkin? It is full of gooey **pulp**. There are also lots and lots of seeds.

Chapter 2

Growing Pumpkins

This teeny plant is called a sprout.

How do pumpkins grow? Seeds are planted in the spring. The seeds grow into little plants that poke through the ground.

The flower looks like this up close.

This is a vine.

The plants keep growing until they are long and twisty. Now they are called vines. The vines have pretty yellow flowers.

Fun Fact

Pumpkins need both sun and water to grow.

Some of the flowers turn into baby pumpkins. In summer, the pumpkins are green and tiny. But each day they get a little bigger.

Pumpkins grow in a pumpkin patch.

In fall, the pumpkins are all grown up. They are also bright orange and ready to pick!

Chapter 3

Pumpkin Treats

It is fun to go pumpkin picking in the fall. There are so many pumpkins! Which one would you choose?

Fun Fact

People use pumpkins to make bread, muffins, soup, and ice cream.

There are lots of things you can do with pumpkins. You can make a pumpkin pie. Mmmm!

You can bake the seeds in the oven for a crunchy treat.

A pumpkin with a carved face is called a jack-o'-lantern.

You can even carve a pumpkin face. It can be scary or super silly. Wow! Pumpkins are one perfect fruit!

Glossary

gourd (**gord**): a type of fruit that includes pumpkins, squash, cucumbers, and melons

jack-o'-lantern: (**jak**-uh-lan-turn) a pumpkin with a face carved in it

lopsided (**lop**-**sye**-did): when one side of something is bigger than the other

pulp (**puhlp**): the soft, juicy part of a fruit

sprout (**sprout**): a tiny, new plant

vine (**vine**): a plant with a long, twisting stem

Comprehension Questions

1. Can you name one thing that you find inside a pumpkin?
2. Can you name two things you can do with a pumpkin?
3. Can you share three more facts about pumpkins?